THE BEST
CATS
EVER

SPHYNX ARE THE BEST!

Elaine Landau

LERNER PUBLICATIONS COMPANY · MINNEAPOLIS

Lerner Publications Company
A division of Lerner Publishing Group, Inc.
241 First Avenue North
Minneapolis, MN 55401 U.S.A.

Website address: www.lernerbooks.com

Library of Congress Cataloging-in-Publication Data

Landau, Elaine.
    Sphynx are the best! / by Elaine Landau.
        p.   cm. — (The best cats ever)
    Includes index.
    ISBN 978-0-7613-6429-0 (lib. bdg. : alk. paper)
    1. Sphynx cat—Juvenile literature. I. Title.
SF449.S68L36 2011
636.8-dc22   2010028472

Manufactured in the United States of America
1 — CG — 12/31/10

TABLE OF CONTENTS

CHAPTER ONE

WHERE'S THE HAIR?

I'm thinking of a special cat. This curious kitty is not like most felines. Some cats have long, fluffy coats. Other cats have hair that's nice and short. But the **sphynx** is almost hairless. At first, you might not think it looks like a cat at all.

Sphynx cats stand out in a crowd. These cats have only a thin layer of hair, usually on their noses, tails, and feet. The body of a sphynx feels like a warm, fuzzy peach.

NAMING YOUR SPHYNX

The sphynx is a special cat. Give it a special NAME. Do any of these fit your furless friend?

Baldy

Grace

Molly

Wrinkles

Harry

E.T.

PEACH

Harriet

Manny

Slinky

Not Too Big

The sphynx is a medium-sized cat. It has huge ears and a long, slim tail. A typical female sphynx weighs about 7 pounds (3 kilograms). Males are a little larger than females. An adult male sphynx weighs about 9 pounds (4 kg).

It's easy to tell a sphynx (right) from most other cats. The sphynx doesn't have heavy fur like the cat on the left.

Colorful Kitties

Sphynx cats come in many colors, such as orange, white, and sandy brown. A sphynx can have spots or patterns on its skin too. Some of these cats look like they have tattoos!

Each of these cats is a different color, but they are all sphynx cats.

Are these kitties pretty?
It depends on whom you ask.
Some people think sphynx
cats are beautiful. Others say
they look like small, wrinkled aliens.
You'll have to judge for yourself.

A Super Show Cat

Do you want a feline that you can enter in cat shows? Sphynx cats are natural show-offs. They enjoy being the center of attention. Judges find them easy to handle. Crowds think they're fun to look at too. Sphynx cats often leave the show ring with top honors.

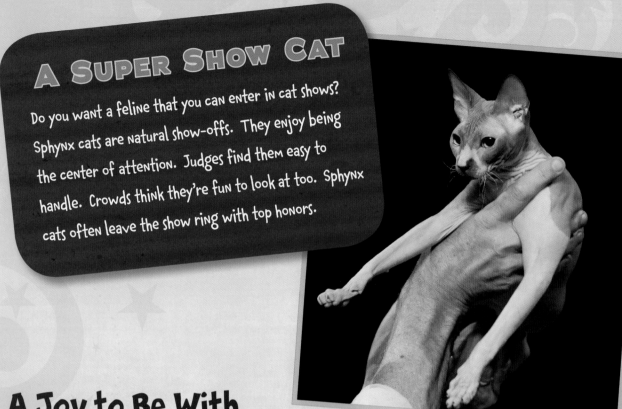

A Joy to Be With

The sphynx is more than just an unusual-looking cat. It's also a great animal to have around. These cats are very intelligent. They learn their names quickly and come when called. Some even learn to do tricks or walk on a leash. Sphynx cats also have lots of energy. Many enjoy games of fetch.

Both of these sphynx cats love to hang out on their owners' shoulders!

Sphynx cats are friendly and loving as well. A sphynx just loves to snuggle. You'll often find a sphynx sitting in its owner's lap or curled around its owner's neck. Their owners think they have the best cats ever!

THE STORY BEHIND THE SPHYNX

Just look at a sphynx. You can tell that it's a special kind of kitty. This unusual cat has an interesting history too.

Bald kitties have shown up here and there for more than a century. By the early 1900s, a few people reported such cats in Europe, Australia, and the United States. But bald kittens were very rare. There was no such thing as a "hairless" breed yet.

Nellie and Dick are two of the earliest-known hairless cats. A man from New Mexico received them from Native Americans in the area.

The Birth of a Breed

Then, in 1966, a short-haired cat in Toronto, Canada, produced a special litter. The litter had a hairless cat in it. This wrinkled little kitten was named Prune.

Prune became part of a new breeding program. Breeders hoped to create a breed of hairless cats. But the program didn't go well. The kittens were born with serious health problems.

Cat breeds called the donskoy (below) and the peterbald (right) look similar to the sphynx.

RUSSIAN HAIRLESS CATS

The sphynx is also known as the Canadian hairless. This is because some of the very first sphynx cats came from Canada. In the 1980s and 1990s, new breeds of hairless cats appeared in Russia. They were the donskoy and the peterbald. These breeds look a bit like the sphynx, but the sphynx is not related to them.

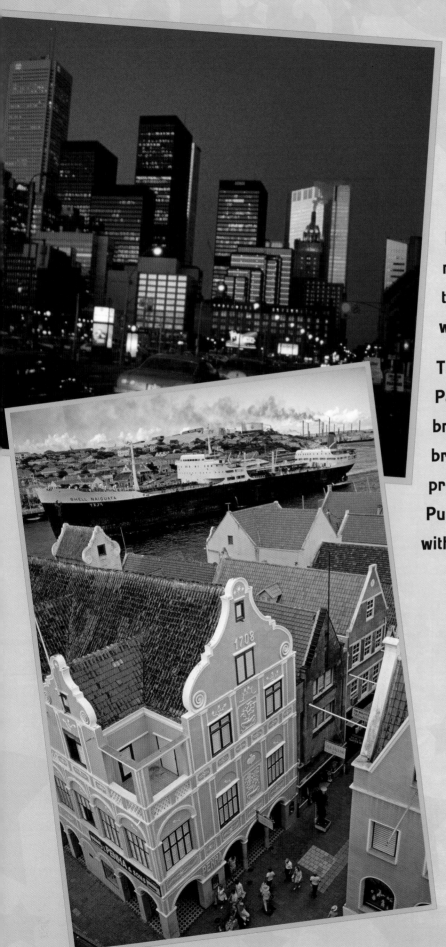

In the 1970s, three other hairless cats were found on the streets of Toronto. Some people believed the cats were related to Prune. One of the cats was male. Two were female.

The females, Punkie and Paloma, were sent to a breeder in Holland. The breeder hoped to safely produce a hairless breed. Punkie and Paloma bred with European cats.

Punkie and Paloma traveled from Toronto (top) to Holland (left) to be bred safely.

In 1975, another hairless kitten was born in Minnesota. Its mother was a short-haired brown tabby named Jezabelle. The next year, Jezabelle gave birth to one more hairless kitten. These cats, along with the hairless felines from Europe, were the start of a new breed. Breeders named it the sphynx.

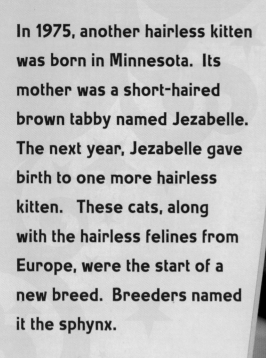

This sphynx cat is dressed up like an Egyptian! Egyptians built the Sphinx sculpture (below).

Is the Sphynx Like the Sphinx?

The sphynx cat isn't from Egypt. But it is named after a famous Egyptian sculpture. The Great Sphinx of Giza has a lion's body and a human's head. This sculpture is much older than the sphynx cat. The Egyptians built it more than four thousand years ago!

Not an Instant Hit

Not everyone liked the sphynx. Some people thought these "naked" cats looked funny. Others thought they looked sickly. And at first, many sphynx cats did have health problems. But breeders worked very hard to make this breed healthy and sweet. Soon sphynx cats found lots of fans!

The sphynx has slowly become a cat many people love.

CHAPTER
THREE

THE SPHYNX AND YOU

You're set on a sphynx. You've become a big fan of these fun, wrinkly cats. You've just got to get one of your own.

But wait! Don't rush out to get a sphynx just yet. Is it really the right kitty for you?

This Cat Needs Company

Sphynx cats adore being with their owners. They love being part of the household action. Your sphynx might follow you from room to room. It will purr and nudge you to get your attention.

Sphynx cats love attention from their owners.

Be prepared to spend lots of time with your sphynx. These cats need to be played with. Do you have lots of after-school activities? Are you busy with your friends most weekends? If so, the sphynx might not be the best cat for you.

Do You Have Allergies?

People with cat allergies are sometimes drawn to the sphynx. They think they'll be fine with a hairless cat. But sphynx cats produce a substance that causes allergic reactions. It's in their saliva (the clear fluid in a cat or person's mouth). Although some people with allergies are OK around a sphynx, many are not.

An Indoor-Only Cat

Don't plan to go on picnics with your sphynx. These cats should not be allowed to play outside. Sphynx sunburn easily. And they can get chilly very quickly in cold weather. Keep your sphynx indoors where it's safe and warm.

Sphynx cats aren't crazy about the cold. This sphynx wears a sweater to stay comfy.

Sphynx Cats Are Expensive

Sphynx are purebred cats. They are also fairly rare. Breeders often ask a lot of money for their kittens. A sphynx may cost hundreds or even thousands of dollars. Can your family afford a pricey pet? Be sure to discuss this with them.

A sphynx kitten (right) can cost a lot of money. Older cats like the twelve-year-old sphynx below are often less expensive.

RESCUE A SPHYNX

Want a sphynx but can't afford one? How about getting an older cat instead of a kitten? Many older sphynx cats can be found at rescue centers for this breed. Often you can get one for a low fee. Just remember: All cats are expensive. Even if you don't pay much for your new pet, your family will still need to spend money on food and health care. But adopting a rescue cat can help you cut down on the purchase price.

Have you decided if the sphynx is right for you? If it is, you've made a great choice. These cats are supersweet and loving. Enjoy your new best friend!

CHAPTER FOUR

WELCOME YOUR SPHYNX

You woke up this morning with a big smile on your face. The day you've waited for is here. You're bringing your sphynx home.

This baby sphynx was just born!

Be Prepared

You want everything to be perfect. You've already got your camera out, but you'll need more than that. Here's a starter list of supplies every sphynx owner should have:

- food and water bowls

- cat food

- litter box

- kitty litter

- warm cat sweater (for colder days indoors)

- scratching post

- cat carrier

Get to a Vet

Take your cat to a veterinarian soon.
That's a doctor who takes care of
animals. They are called vets for short.

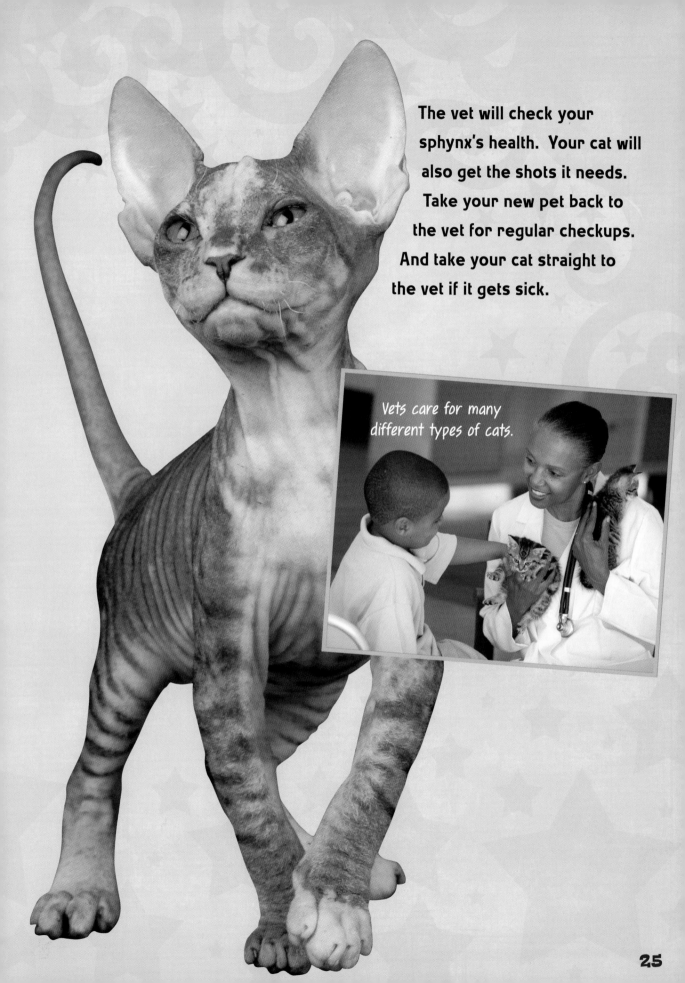

The vet will check your sphynx's health. Your cat will also get the shots it needs. Take your new pet back to the vet for regular checkups. And take your cat straight to the vet if it gets sick.

Vets care for many different types of cats.

What's for Dinner?

Cats need different food at different times in their lives. Ask your vet what to feed your kitty. And stick to cat food. An overweight cat is an unhealthy cat. Don't sneak your sphynx table scraps.

A REFRESHING DRINK

Water is as important as the right diet to your pet's health. Your vet is sure to agree! Make sure your sphynx always has fresh, cool water in a clean bowl.

Bath Time

Your sphynx may not have a long coat, but it still needs your help staying clean. Most sphynx cats need a bath about once a week. Bathing keeps a sphynx's skin healthy. You should also clean your cat's ears weekly.

You and Your Sphynx

The sphynx is a great cat. If you have one, you're really lucky. Make your cat feel lucky to have you too. Be your cat's best friend. Give your sphynx the love and the attention it needs.

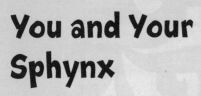

Do You Feel Chilly?

If you're cold, chances are your sphynx is too. Sometimes these cats need their owners' help to stay warm. Make a place for your cat in front of a sunny window. You can also find heated pet beds at some pet stores. Many sphynx cats are quite fond of these beds.

Remember to feed and pet your sphynx even when you're tired or busy. You just may have the best cat ever. So be the best owner you can be. Your sphynx will repay you with loads of love!

GLOSSARY

breed: a particular type of cat. Cats of the same breed have the same body shape and general features. *Breed* can also refer to producing kittens.

breeder: someone who mates cats to produce a particular type of cat

coat: a cat's fur

diet: the food your cat eats

feline: a cat, or having to do with cats

litter: a group of kittens born to one mother

purebred: a cat whose parents are of the same breed

rescue center: a shelter where stray and abandoned cats are kept until they are adopted

saliva: the clear fluid in a cat or person's mouth

sculpture: something carved or shaped out of stone, wood, or another firm material

veterinarian: a doctor who treats animals. Veterinarians are called vets for short.

FOR MORE INFORMATION

Books

Brecke, Nicole, and Patricia M. Stockland. *Cats You Can Draw*. Minneapolis: Millbrook Press, 2010. Perfect for cat lovers, this colorful book teaches readers how to draw many popular cat breeds, including the sphynx.

Brown, Ruth. *Gracie the Lighthouse Cat*. London: Andersen Press, 2011. Gracie the lighthouse cat and Grace Darling, the lighthouse keeper's daughter, both have an adventure one very windy night.

Harris, Trudy. *Tally Cat Keeps Track*. Minneapolis: Millbrook Press, 2011. Tally McNally is a cat who loves to tally—but one day, he gets into a jam. Will his friends find a way to help him?

Hengel, Katherine. *Smooth Sphynx*. Edina, MN: ABDO Publishing, 2010. Check out this book for more information about the sphynx's body basics and loving personality.

Landau, Elaine. *Your Pet Cat*. Rev. ed. New York: Children's Press, 2007. This title is a good guide for young people on choosing and caring for a cat.

Websites

ASPCA Kids
http://www.aspca.org/aspcakids
Check out this website for helpful hints on caring for a cat and other pets.

For Kids: About Cats
http://kids.cfa.org
Be sure to visit this website on cats and cat shows. Don't miss the link to some fun games as well.

Sphynx Cat Breed Rescues
http://purebredcats.org/sphynx.htm
This nationwide nonprofit group helps sphynx cats find loving homes.

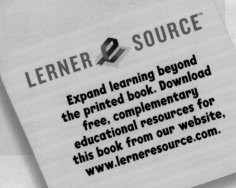

LERNER e SOURCE™

Expand learning beyond the printed book. Download free, complementary educational resources for this book from our website, www.lernerresource.com.

Index

Photo Acknowledgments

The images in this book are used with the permission of: backgrounds © iStockphoto.com/javarman3 and © iStockphoto.com/Julie Fisher; © iStockphoto.com/Michael Balderas, p. 1; © Lincurrie/Dreamstime.com, pp. 4, 15 (top); © Gandee Vasan/Stone/Getty Images, p. 5; © Eric Isselée/Dreamstime.com, pp. 6 (top), 20 (bottom); © Krissilundgren/Dreamstime.com, p. 6 (middle); © Kirill Vorobyev/Shutterstock Images, p. 6 (bottom); © Juniors Bildarchiv/Alamy, p. 7; © Samuel Kubani/AFP/Getty Images, p. 8 (top); © Photos by Dana/Flickr/Getty Images, p. 8 (bottom); © NY Daily News/Getty Images, p. 9 (top); © Jack Guez/AFP/Getty Images, p. 9 (bottom); © Krissi Lundgren/Alamy, p. 10; © Emprise/Dreamstime.com, p. 11 (left); Frances Simpson, *The Book of the Cat*, Cassell and Company, 1903, p. 11 (right); © Ekaterina Cherakashina/Dreamstime.com, p. 12 (left); © Natalia Belotelova/Dreamstime.com, p. 12 (right); © Robert Estall/CORBIS, p. 13 (top); © Emory Kristof/National Geographic/Getty Images, p. 13 (bottom); © Charles Eshelman/FilmMagic/Getty Images, p. 14 (top); © Albo/Dreamstime.com, p. 14 (bottom); © iStockphoto.com/Alexander Perl, p. 15 (bottom); © Fiona Green, pp. 16, 18 (top), 21 (bottom), 23 (top), 24, 26, 27 (left), 29; © Eric Isselée/Shutterstock Images, p. 18 (bottom); © Juice Team/Shutterstock Images, pp. 17, 21 (top); © LinnCurrie/Dreamstime.com, p. 19 (top); © RIA Novosti/TopFoto/The Image Works, p. 19 (bottom); © Anna Utekhina/Dreamstime.com, p. 20 (top); © iStockphoto.com/Alexander Perl, p. 22; © Richard Nelson/Dreamstime.com, p. 23 (middle); © Eti Swinford/Dreamstime.com, p. 23 (bottom left); © Mike Bond/Dreamstime.com, p. 23 (bottom right); © Dobermanstudio/Dreamstime.com, p. 25 (left); © Blend Images/Getty Images, p. 25 (right); © Roberto della vite/MARKA/Alamy, p. 27 (right); © Dracorubio Images/Flickr/Getty Images, p. 28 (top); © iStockphoto.com/Ruth Ann Johnston, p. 28 (bottom).

Front cover: © Juniors Bildarchiv/Alamy.
Back cover: © Kirill Vorobyev/Shutterstock Images.